A Cheese Sandwich for John Lennon

Coming of Age in Rockin' Liverpool!

by

Maire E. McMahon

Editing and Cover Design by Jason Rosette

'A Cheese Sandwich for John Lennon: Coming of Age in Rockin' Liverpool!'

Published by Oscar Enterprises, Ltd.

Visit www.maireemcmahon.com for more information and to contact the author

To all my friends in Liverpool...

TABLE OF CONTENTS

BUDDY HOLLY COMES
TO BALA STREET

Jive, bop, call it what you like, it was the dance that my best friend Bernie taught me in her front parlor. We were first introduced to American Rock n' Roll by the way of Buddy Holly records in the nineteen fifties, when we were both fifteen years old. We took to this strange new music right away and soon began to hold impromptu dance and shuffle sessions despite all the effort it took to get our hands on a record player.

Bernie lived on the same street as me, but her house was halfway up the hill and located directly next to the only lamppost on the block. Though her house was also close to one of three large sewage drains in our street, it was at times the best of locations when her family ran out of shillings to put into the 'lecky' meter. In such an instance, the streetlamp shone into their house providing them with some light during those lean times.

On the other hand, Bernie's house became a grim place to live when debris blocked the storm drain after a heavy downpour. When that happened, grease-soaked newspaper wrappings from fish and chip dinners, gnawed and discarded dog-bones, cigarette stubs, and the occasional beer bottle lodged amid nature's flotsam of twigs and leaves. Swept down the hill, it became trapped on the grating where the vile heap would finally come to rest in front of her house. The resulting mess invariably attracted large rats from surrounding city sewers but there was nothing to be done besides beating the vermin away with a large stick, then waiting until the '*corpy*' sent workers to unclog the drain.

One spring evening we sat together on the curb, our feet on the grid which smelled decent in cool weather, passing time by teasing Bernie's dog Blackie. We had slung a rope across the arms of the lamppost, then tied a bone to the other end to keep it just out of the dog's reach. Blackie jumped into the air again and again, snapping each time at the speedily retracted treat, which made us giggle each time he failed to reach the target.

Our laughter was interrupted by the sudden sound of music coming from Bernie's front parlor. We could tell right away that it was music from America. It was the distinctive sound of guitars squealing, and the pleasant drawl of the singer that gave it away.

"Which radio station is that music coming from?" I asked.

Bernie shook her head, "Not coming from a radio station."

"Then where's it coming from?"

"Ye'll have to wait and see." she replied, wearing a mischievous grin. "It's a surprise. Come inside and I'll show you!"

We extracted our feet from the sewage grid and removed the rope from the lamppost just as the song came to an end. After a slight pause the exact song began to play for a second time.

"That's funny," I commented, "it's that guy singing again." We heard a giggle and turned to see Bernie's sister standing in the doorway with a big smile on her face.

"Alright Rita, what's happening? Are you going to let on?"

Her grin grew bigger. She was very chuffed, pleased at keeping me in suspense.

Rita was only two years older than Bernie and I, but she was way ahead of us in maturity. She looked grown up already, with delicate features and glorious auburn curls which accentuated her milk-white skin. And she was ambitious! Not only did she have a full-time job at Littlewoods Football Pool Company, but in her spare time, she ran a shopping catalogue selling glamorous lingerie and household items throughout our neighborhood.

Her product line included those pointy bras that all the American movie stars wore, as well as Max Factor Pancake makeup from Hollywood, and small electric appliances such as irons, vacuum cleaners, and record players. Rita often allowed Bernie and I to browse the pages and sometimes, even let us order small items on the *'never, never'* owing a shilling a week until fully paid. Now she was inviting us to inspect her latest treasure.

"Come and have a look at my new record player!"

"Go wan! You haven't got one of those, have you?"

In response, Rita grabbed my arm and dragged me into the small parlor room where a shiny square box sat on the sideboard.

"Isn't it smashing?" declared Bernie proudly.

"Yea, not half!" I answered. "Who's that singing?"

"It's Buddy Holly from America", came the answer.

"That's a funny name for a bloke, isn't it?" I replied. "And what's the song called?"

"'Peggy Sue! It's a big hit in New York."

I listened intently, not yet sure if I liked this strange but fascinating new American song. I already loved listening to Louis Armstrong's jazz, Patsy Cline's country music, and Judy Garland's Broadway show songs on BBC radio, but I had never heard anything like this.

"Where did it all come from?" I asked.

"I bought the record player from my catalogue, and a feller I work with sold me the record. His brother sails on the Sylvania and brings bags full of them back from New York every couple of weeks."

"Ah well," I said, "now I see your plan."

Many young Liverpool lads joined the Merchant navy. It was a chance to see the world, and it paid a lot better than factory work. Aspiring sailors took an exam at sixteen and if they passed, they could sign on with a ship going back and forth from Liverpool to New York. While the cargo or passengers were being unloaded, the lads would be free to roam around the city to sightsee a bit along Broadway. On their way back to the ship, they would fill their kit bags with records and blue jeans and other 'American stuff' which they could sell once they returned home, making a little extra cash.

Entranced by this new contraption, we three girls sat replaying the Buddy Holly record over and over. When it came to an end, we lifted the needle to replay it until we had learned the words. We sang along in unison:

"I love you Peggy Sue
With a heart so rare and true,
Oh Peggy, my Peggy Sue,
Pretty, pretty, pretty, pretty Peggy Sue!

We giggled at the words as we sang, until the shilling ran out in the electric meter. The record came to a slow, slurring halt and the lights went out all through the house. Bernie's mother, Mrs. Murphy, shouted down the stairs for Rita to *stop using up the lecky with that bloody thing!*

The two sisters and I trooped outside to continue our discussion by the light of the streetlamp.

"So, Rita. Is this real rock n' roll music?"

"Yes, the real thing. Straight from the US of A!"

"Can we dance to this?"

"Yea, all the young ones are doing it. ITV has a program on television every Saturday night at six o'clock. They play the latest hit-songs, and they invite teenagers onto the stage to dance rock n' roll."

"Ah, but no one in this street has a television set."

"Mrs. Jones has just got one. You two should go and ask her if she would let you come in and watch the dance show."

"Do you think...she would let us?"

"Yea, I think so. She let all the neighborhood kids go in last Wednesday night to watch *Wagon Train*."

But I was too impatient to wait until Saturday.

"Do you know any of the steps Rita?" I asked.

"Yes, I learned some at Littlewoods social club. It's easy! Come on Bernie. I'll teach you first while Maire watches."

The pair of them stood under the yellow light of the lamp facing each other while holding hands. Rita began to twirl Bernie around and they started singing *Peggy Sue*. I joined in singing to create a beat as the two danced faster.

Alarmed at the antics of the two sisters, stray dogs barked frantically up and down the street, and lights went on in the front rooms of a couple of neighborhood houses. Round and round the sisters danced. Rita even began to shake her hips. I watched from my seat on the front step, carefully studying the moves before getting up to join them.

Mrs. Coldtart, a neighbor who lived across the street from Bernie, came to stand at her front door. She watched for about five minutes while we danced, before shouting across the street to us.

"That's bloody disgusting that is!" she screamed in her shrill, street seller voice.

"Youse lot should be ashamed of yerselves, gyrating yer bodies like strip tease dancers."

"It's not as bad as the Charleston, Missus," responded Bernie, without pausing her gyrations.

"Aye aye! Enough of that cheek." It was Bernie's mother, Mrs. Murphy, calling from inside the house. "Get inside the house Bernie, and you get yourself home Maire. Rita you'd better go up to the Eagle & Child and get us a couple of shillings for the meter so your dad can have a cuppa when he gets home from work."

Our impromptu dance lesson had ended for the night...but our ongoing plans for dancing had just begun.

It was I who had been nominated to talk to Mrs. Jones, owner of the only television set in the neighborhood. Gaining access to her TV was the only way we could watch the six o'clock Rock n' Roll show on Saturday, so this was a crucial mission. I decided to go the following day.

As I arrived at Mrs. Jones' house, I noticed the front door had been left unlocked and ajar: there seemed to be nobody home. I knocked anyway and waited. There was no response. *'She has probably gone grocery shopping',* I thought. My mouth was dry, and my stomach fluttered, but I knew I had to give it a solid effort before returning home.

I cleared my throat: "Are you in there, Mrs. Jones?" I called into the deserted lobby. "It's me, Maire Mac from across the street."

I waited, listening in silence for a response. Not a peep. I waited a few more minutes and was about to turn away, when I could faintly discern the sounds of footsteps descending the creaking stairs. Then a man's voice responded from behind a closed door somewhere in the house.

"Hang on there luv, I'll be down in a minute."

A minute passed, then another. Ten minutes went by before the lobby door finally opened, and there stood a disheveled Mr. Jones. His uncombed hair made him appear as though he had jumped out of bed and straight into his clothes.

"Well, 'ello there, girl," he said as he looked me up and down. A bent grin crept across his face before he spoke again.

"Come in and have a cup of tea. Keep me company until the missus gets back in five minutes."

Now I was in a pickle! I couldn't go inside the house because he made me nervous, but I still needed to complete my assignment.

"I've got to babysit in a minute," I said, "but just came to ask Mrs. Jones if I could come Saturday to watch the six o'clock music show on your telly."

"Well, ye can ask me luv, it's my telly as well."

"Would you let a couple of us come over for an hour to watch the music show on Saturday? We need to learn the latest dance moves."

"Of course, darlin, but ye'll have to save a dance for me!" he replied with a hoarse giggle, which quickly evolved into a fit of coughing.

"Alright." I answered hurriedly. "We'll be seeing you at six on Saturday then."

I raced away up the street as fast as I could and banged on Bernie's door. It opened immediately and she beckoned me inside.

"We're on for Saturday night at Mrs. Jones house - "

Bernie began to clap her hands together but paused when she noticed the look of concern on my face indicating that I had more to say.

"...but we have to save a dance for her mister. He was the only one home, so I had to ask him. And that's the deal."

"Ugh, that old lech!" said Bernie. "He's so creepy."

"We just won't show up." I offered.

"Ah no, we'll be fine. He'll behave himself while his missus is watching." She began to giggle, adding, "Besides, we can handle him."

We counted the days until Saturday, and at five minutes to six in the evening, Bernie and I knocked at the Joneses front door. I heard high-heeled shoes pounding heavily down the lobby, and the door flew open to reveal Mrs. Jones all dressed up in her best outfit, ready for an evening out. Now I was worried again. Was she leaving us alone with her dubious husband? Should we turn around before it was too late? Trust my friend Bernie to lead the way.

"Don't ye' look grand, Mrs. Jones," Bernie remarked with a smile as she strode into the house. "Gorgeous as usual."

"I'll have none of yer ould gab, Bernie Murphy! Ye've got a cheek working yer way in to watch the television when me and the ould feller had other plans for tonight."

Bernie's sudden confidence fled as she deflated and spun around towards the door.

"Sorry about that. We'll be on our way then." she said.

Mrs. Jones blocked the door.

"I'll let it be this time. But just this once and no more!" she said, waving us through to the room where the new contraption sat waiting.

Mr. Jones sat by the fireplace drinking a glass of Mackeson's stout. He beckoned us to sit down.

"Hurry up now. The show has already begun."

Shy and speechless for the moment, Bernie and I took our seats on the sofa in front of the shimmering new television set. We watched as the onscreen stage revolved, and a skiffle group appeared with the drummer seated and ready to play.

Mrs. Jones was relaxing now, after having quickly swallowing her glass of brown ale. She stood to get a refill then changed her mind, stopping to pull Mr. Jones onto his feet. *"The Rock Island Line is a mighty fine line…"* she sang loudly along with the skiffle group, while swinging her husband around the room.

"I luv this song!" she announced, releasing her grip on her husband to twirl around in a world of her own. Mister Jones took the opportunity to discreetly escape, leaving his wife in a solo performance.

"I wouldn't wanna guess how many she's had before we got here, but she's well soused." Bernie whispered in my ear.

Every so often she would do a high kick, lifting her leg in the air to point her toes like a ballerina.

Bernie egged her on.

"Sure, and it's hard not to fancy we're in the Follies Bergère in Paris! Such an expert dancer you are Mrs. Jones."

She stopped dancing for a moment and looked directly at Bernie, briefly terrorizing us, before reaching for my friend's hand.

"Come on, girl. I'll show you how it's done."

As they danced together, I noticed from my seat on the couch, that Bernie looked like an adult. She had grown taller, and now broader in the shoulders than Mrs. Jones. The music stopped and a young male singer was introduced to the audience. He began to sing quietly: *"Oh, Rose Marie I love you, I'm always thinking of you...*" It was a romantic song, ideal for a slow dance but to my horror I realized that I was alone while Bernie and Mrs. Jones were busy dancing in the kitchen. Sure enough, there came Mr. Jones making a direct line to me, defenseless on the sofa.

"I'm 'ere to claim me prize luv," he announced while reaching for my hand. "I luv Slim Whitman singing this one," he added, pulling me like a rag doll to my feet.

Working for years as a longshoreman, he had developed a grip like a clamp, so it was no use struggling. He began singing along while squeezing himself up against me, ready to settle in for a few minutes of an 'up close encounter'. I wondered how I might pry myself loose when Bernie suddenly appeared and cut in, taking Mr. Jones hand in a sort of self-sacrifice for my sake.

"My turn luv!" she shouted over the din of the combined sounds of the television, the high-pitched voice of Mrs. Jones singing in the kitchen, and the gravelly sounds coming from her husband. Bernie twirled her new partner around, creating a chance for me to break free of the old longshoreman's grip. No sooner had I stumbled free, however, than I found myself in the kitchen hand in hand with Mrs. Jones, who now began to teach me the same dance moves she had just bestowed upon Bernie.

Finally, our fit of dancing subsided, and we made our way back to the sofa and sat again in front of the marvelous new TV to catch the rest of the show. We watched young British singers perform hit songs from the Top Twenty that had been sung originally by

American groups. We heard the familiar strains of such tunes as: Frankie Lyman and the Teenagers' "Why Do Fools Fall in Love?", and Gene Vincent's 'Be Bop a Lula". The show concluded with a lovely rendition of The Everly Brothers, "Bye, bye Love".

No sooner had the last strains of music subsided than Mrs. Jones snapped off the TV, leaving a small fading dot in the center of the polished tube. "Alright, you two, be off with ye now," ordered Mrs. Jones, "and don't come back next week!"

"Ah now," answered Bernie, "we were planning to come next Wednesday night for *Wagon Train*!"

Mr. Jones seemed to find the idea agreeable, and that strange grin appeared on his face again...but his Missus would have none of it.

"No youse don't," Mrs. Jones shouted, "that show's just for the kiddies, not for cheeky teenagers like you, Bernie Murphy!"

I intervened diplomatically.

"Well, thanks for teaching us the steps, Mrs. Jones. You're a smashing dancer."

She turned to look at me, her face softening for a split second. Was she about to change her mind and let us come again next week? But her eyes quickly narrowed again.

"Ah, yer getting as bad as this friend of yours, Bernie Murphy. On yer way, the two of ye and don't come back!"

She then ushered us out, with Mr. Jones waving a faint goodbye behind us, with his glass of Mackie's stout in hand. The front door thudded shut leaving us alone in the darkened street.

Despite the abrupt ending, we had succeeded in our mission! We had gained access to Mrs. Jones' newfangled television, and we had managed to watch nearly the entire music program while learning some new dance moves on the side.

There was a nice moon out, and the sky was full of stars as we walked slowly up the hill to Bernie's house. We talked nonstop on the way, going back over and reviewing all that we had seen and heard for that single hour on the television. It was an exciting time for us, as we felt that our lives seemed to have taken a turn for the better in a single night.

There was a promising world opening for us; at least that's what it felt like. It was as if the old, grey Liverpool of the Blitz had stepped aside slightly, to make room for a new kind of city in a new kind of world. A world with music for our generation with new ways of dancing. New fashions were showing up in the shops, bringing new colors and styles.

Although Bernie and I were only fifteen, and still too young to go dancing at the big ballrooms, we were determined to build on our evening's experience...

Like butterflies, we were preparing ourselves to emerge fully mature and developed. We would practice our dancing and study the new styles. We would play records and memorize the words until the gramophone needles grew dull. We would someday, not too far off in the future, shuffle off our former chrysalis, the drib-drab lives we had known before, to fly beyond the horizon.

LAST WALTZ AT
CAMPBELL'S DANCE SCHOOL

Wearing my sister Joan's high-heeled shoes, I wobbled along Old Barn Road on my way to dancing class. The street was an obstacle course, no place to dawdle and daydream if I were to avoid craggy gaps in the broken cement and the numerous piles of dog poo scattered across my path. It would not do to traipse into Campbell's School of Ballroom Dance, with only one high-heeled shoe, or with a clump of dog poo stuck to my shoe - or both! I imagined with a wicked smile that it might be a good solution to this dancing school problem, if I were to be banned from the dreaded academy. It had been Ma's idea anyway. She had set her heart on the idea that dancing would magically transform me from a teenage ruffian into a lady. Blaming my rough and ready disposition on the war, she was determined to polish me up, such that I might become acceptably genteel.

My parents did not plan to bring another child into the world during a war and they were quite put out when Chamberlain failed to reach an agreement with Hitler. I was born a few months before the 1940 bombing of Liverpool, when the Luftwaffe pounded the city throughout the autumn months. As luck would have it, my Uncle Billy's large family of nine came to live in our tiny house in Huyton Village where my family had recently been resettled, escaping the rubble of their dockside home.

Ma had mixed feelings about this turn of events as she watched her two-bedroom home become packed with old army cots, then filled with children who slept crosswise, head to tail, like sardines in a can. And all those extra mouths to feed! Yet on the other hand, she realized that there was an endless supply of eager minders for the new baby.

Other adults in the household also realized that the small house was unable to contain all that childish energy during the day, so they quickly weeded out those who were too small to work in the vegetable garden, or too puny to turn the wheel on the laundry wringing-machine. Then we little ones were thus sent outside to fend for ourselves until dusk, and Lord Derby's nearby estate became the destination for our playful games and frolicking, our second home (while the Lord himself was away) with its private forest of trees to climb and streams to jump.

After the war, Uncle Billy's family returned to the city, and Ma decided that it was time for us all to get back to 'civilized activities'. Worried that, if left to my own devices, I might end up becoming a Red Beret in the British Army, or a high wire act in a travelling circus, she dragged me along to church and enrolled me in the Girl Guides. They quickly dis-enrolled me due to my lack of girlish ways, considering me coarse as the coal from our black iron fire grate. Undeterred, Ma then tried to install me in a local theatrical troupe, followed by a country dancing group - to no avail. Not a grain of culture could they detect in my happy go lucky soul! Now that I was a teenager, Campbell's School of Ballroom Dance became Ma's last resort. It was the final, hopeful sanctum of civility to which I headed on a Monday evening after work.

When I arrived at the end of Old Barn Road, I turned left onto Breck Road, passing the library which had been 'temporarily' housed for the past ten years in an ugly, prefabricated structure on a battered plot where its grand predecessor had stood before the Blitz. I took a right turn at Holy Trinity Church which, despite its sinister black-spired, Victorian exterior, everyone 'C of E' (Church of England) in the neighborhood flocked for their baptismal, marriage and funeral ceremonies.

Ambling reluctantly along Ambrose Grove, I approached an old Victorian house at the end of the cul-de-sac. A steady stream of teenagers from across the City of Liverpool milled about in the street in front of me, eager to fork over their tuition fee at the door in exchange for the renowned expertise of the elderly dancing champions inside.

Campbell's was a bit of a finishing school for working class kids like me, who left school at fifteen to labor in grimy factories. I considered myself lucky when hired to work at a local chocolate factory, whose 'perks' allowed me to eat as much chocolate as I could tolerate. Although our scholastic dreams had been temporarily nipped in the bud, we knew that learning how to dance could help us enter an adult world with our manners somewhat polished up...and who knew? At the dance class, we might happen upon a Prince Charming who could whisk us away from lives working at the conveyor belt.

Mr. and Mrs. Campbell waited to welcome us in front of open French doors whose glass panes, age-worn and marred by cracks, mirrored the faces of the old champions. Former sylph-like figures, now softened by the passing years into plumpness and tango-tired legs supported by elastic stockings, the couple appeared as a still-frame from an old silent movie. Together they stood holding hands while their poker-straight bodies formed a barrier, controlling who could enter their beloved ballroom.

Their vintage finery bristled in anticipation of the evening's activities. Mr. Campbell with hair worn in a British Army short-back-and-sides regulation cut, had on shiny, patent-leather dancing shoes, which complimented a well-worn tuxedo. His wife wore a taffeta and tulle ballerina-length gown, accented by an antique seed-pearl pearl necklace around her neck. Her black, tinted Marcel waved hair sat like an immoveable satin cap on her head.

There was still a shortage of clothing in the city of Liverpool, making it almost impossible to find anything fashionable, but everyone gave it their best effort. My outfit for the evening was a Royal Navy Wrens uniform skirt, purchased for two and sixpence at a military surplus store, then reconstructed in my free time. For weeks I cut and sewed, reworking the coarse fabric into something fashionable. The slinky black result was surprisingly smart and looked especially stylish when worn with a pink, Peter Pan-collared blouse, a black 'waspie' belt - and of course, my older sister Joan's high heeled shoes.

"Come along young people!" bellowed Mr. Campbell in his sergeant major voice, his open palm ready to receive each student's fee of one shilling. "We haven't got all night."

I stood in line behind a group of Teddy Boys about my age. They looked spiffy in their velvet trimmed 'drape' suits, drain-pipe trousers, and fashionably long hair. But trouble loomed as Mrs. Campbell angrily strode in our direction. Squeezing out of line, I quickly relocated myself to a place further down the queue, far enough away from the questionable group of lads to avoid being scooped up in the melee. Ma would batter me if I found myself on the wrong side of the gate, with her final plan for my redemption thwarted.

"On your way young men!" the elderly woman ordered, waving her hand in the air as though fending off a swarm of wasps. The Teddy Boys stirred in an uneasy lump as the queue began to slough them from its coil.

"We don't want your kind here, causing trouble with your gangs and your knuckle dusters. Out!" she shrieked in a high-pitched voice, "before I call the constable!"

Scolded and embarrassed, the group of Teddy Boys slowly retreated, walking back down the path which led to the street accompanied by the sounds of girlish giggling and a few wolf whistles. From the safety of my hide-out in the line, I looked around to see if I recognized anyone. To my horror, I did indeed. It was a white-haired boy who had pursued me briefly in

Country Dance class when we were both students at Stanley Park Secondary School. I had been forced to dance with him, like it or not, because a girl was not allowed to refuse a boy.

He had never uttered a word, not even to ask my name nor to tell me his, so I nicknamed him 'Whitey'. Later, I realized that I should have called him 'Bully', because he seemed to delight in violently pushing me around the floor when we danced the Scottish dance, *The Gay Gordons*. He refused to ask anyone else to dance - I was his sole target, and to add insult to injury, when school ended for the day, he followed me home!

One afternoon during class I plucked up the courage to refuse him. He sat sulking on the bench alone, attracting the attention of the headmistress who promptly disqualified me from the dancing class for displaying 'bad manners'.

Here I was again in the same position: Campbell's School of Dance had the same rule!

Oh god! How can I avoid him now? Maybe I will hide in the toilets until he finds someone else to torment!

I spotted my work friend Nancy at the back of the line and waved frantically for her to join me closer to the front. She always had a solution for everything, and I hoped that she would help me find a way to deal with my undesirable admirer.

She laughed as she flipped the long fringe of hair covering my eyebrows.

"No-one would ever guess that you have only one eyebrow." she remarked with a giggle, referring to an incident which happened the previous week. She had offered to trim my eyebrows, promising that it would help me to look older and 'more glamorous', so I had jumped at the opportunity.

She worked furiously on the left side, plucking the hairs out with tweezers. Suddenly, our supervisor appeared to interrupt the impromptu grooming session.

"'Back on the line you two! It's not break time yet.'"

We skulked away back to work, leaving me with one eyebrow. Days had passed but to my dismay, my eyebrow area was still red and swollen. I was embarrassed to be seen in public but Ma being determined I must go to Campbell's to become more cultured, took a pair of scissors and cut a long fringe of hair which then fell and settled to cover my eyebrows.

True, Nancy had in part caused the 'eyebrow debacle', but I refused to stay angry with her because I liked her so much. She had taken me under her wing like a big sister, teaching me how to dress and socialize for the dance scene. I especially looked forward to her next lesson, in which she promised to teach me how to respond when a boy asked to walk me home!

A large group of grammar school students stood in line ahead of us. Some of the girls looked like bookworms with their greasy, lank hair and government-issue spectacles, while others with bum-high skirts looked fashionable and flirty. The boys were still in uniform with blazers exchanged for sweaters.

There were some young merchant seamen standing proudly behind me, showing off in their new contraband American jeans and at the end of the line I could see funny, handsome Billy Fisher who lived on the next street to mine. He was one of the few people I knew who always had money to spare, probably because he worked for his uncle who sold stuff '*that had fallen off a lorry*' at the back of Paddy's Market.

We moved quickly along until I reached the door where I paid my shilling. Waved inside, I entered the ballroom with a sense of awe. The large room was lit by the northern midsummer light, which shone through a row of French doors on one side of the room, its pale beams coming to rest on the scuffed, oaken boards of the dance floor. Neglected rococo-styled cornices mimicked fabric above the door frames and large, plaster roses decorated the ceiling from whose centers hung dusty, unlit chandeliers.

On the opposite wall, mildewed remnants of silk panels could be seen above chair rails which ran the length of the room. A raised platform at one end of the ballroom held a well-worn, upright piano and a small bamboo table upon which sat a wind-up gramophone.

I recognized the décor of the old mansion as remnants of our glorious Empire. I would not have been surprised to see Miss Havisham, from Charles Dickens's "Great Expectations", seated at the table in her tattered wedding gown. Who could have imagined that, hidden away among the grand old oak trees, just a stone's throw from Freddy the Butchers shop and Sid's pawnbrokers on Breck road, sat this historical gem? Years would pass before I saw anything like it again, and even then, it was only from a distance, when watching a televised tour of Buckingham Palace.

Once inside the ballroom, Mr. and Mrs. Campbell enforced strict rules, beginning with segregation of the sexes. Boys were sent to sit on one side of the room, while girls sat opposite, scrutinizing them from a distance. Only 'gentlemen' could do the inviting, while we girls held our breaths, praying that someone nice would ask us to dance. God forbid if you were the last girl left sitting on the bench facing the one spotty fellow who had not quite warmed to the idea of personal hygiene. Refusal of a partner meant permanent banishment from Campbell's, with the only acceptable excuse being ignorance in failing to know the dance steps. But even that excuse had its penalty!

When a student claimed ignorance or forgetfulness, Mrs. Campbell would briskly scoop up the young man, while Mr. Campbell took his frightened female partner in hand. The gramophone would be wound up as usual, and off they would go, circling counterclockwise around the ballroom at breakneck speed. It was a cross between a slide and a shuffle, following the music of the great Victor Sylvester - *slow, slow, quick, quick, slow* - until Mrs. Campbell caught up with her husband in a passing whoosh of motion. Mr. Campbell would then seamlessly disengage, slinging the girl back towards her original partner. Mission accomplished! The Campbells, with a swish of taffeta and tulle would continue their glide around the floor showing us all how it should be done while the newly instructed couple, like recently hatched fledglings, hesitantly struggled their way along, until the dance ended.

Halfway through the evening we took a rest break, dashing to a side room to buy an orange drink and flirt with the boys. It was our only opportunity, and we had to be quick about it before the Campbells finished their cigarette break outside.

"Can I buy you a Tizer, luv?" came a male voice from behind, along with a tap on the shoulder. I knew only one boy here and turned, expecting to see the white-haired boy from school. Instead, I found myself gazing into a pair of blue, twinkling eyes.

"Oh yes please," I answered in surprise, "thanks, luv."

"Let's stand in the garden, away from the crowd," he suggested as he led the way outside, carrying our drinks.

"Do you come here often?" he asked. His grin caused me to burst into a fit of giggling.

"Can't you think of a better pick-up line than that old raspberry?"

He shrugged sheepishly while I quickly rescued him, replying,

"It's my first time here. What about you?"

"Came here a few times last year before I joined the merch - Merchant Navy I mean. I am Harry by the way. What's your name?"

"Maire." I answered. "Has anyone ever told you that you look just like that film star Richard Widmark who is in all the cowboy movies? Younger though!"

He laughed, but before he could answer, Mrs. Campbell had arrived to break up any budding romances.

"Back to the dance floor ladies and gents. Gird your loins for the Rhumba!"

Harry quickly grabbed my arm. "Save the last waltz for me luv, it's the only dance I know."

"Okay." I answered, before making my way to the long bench where all the girls sat lined up along the wall. I had hoped the white-haired boy would find a new partner today, or perhaps he was still outside because I was unable to see him among the groups of boys. Breathing a sigh of relief, I began to make myself comfortable and to feel optimistic about this dancing business, until there he stood like a statue in front of me.

Expressionless, he stretched out his hand in a silent invitation to dance and there was no way out for me. I had to accept and ruefully rose to walk with him onto the dance floor. We positioned ourselves to dance the Rhumba, exactly how we had been taught by the ancient champions. With his right hand clutched at my waist, the white-haired boy roughly grasped my hand and raised it into the air, Latin style. Then everything fell apart.

No longer following the dance moves, and with thick fingers dug into my arm, the dreaded white-haired boy began mechanically shoving me. Pushing me backwards then pulling forward so rapidly, I almost fell over. The dance was meant to be performed in one small area with the occasional ballerina style twirl but disregarding all instructions about moving to the music and as though maniacally possessed, he shuttled me rapidly around the ballroom. We proceeded to collide with other dancers as we hurtled around the ballroom, leaving a trail of astonished couples in our wake.

Harry stood in the corner watching and grinning. He winked at me sympathetically while I rolled my eyes in despair. Suddenly, strong hands pried me loose from the clutches of the white-haired boy. It was Mr.

Campbell! His bellowing voice resounded across the room, stopping other dancers in their tracks.

"Whoa, young man. Do you think this young lady is a sack of potatoes? Let me show you how to dance the Rhumba!"

I was taken in hand by Mr. Campbell himself, who demanded that Whitey follow us around the floor while he demonstrated the steps to the dance. Under the skillful guidance of the master, I floated effortlessly in circles enjoying myself, relieved to be freed at last from the brutal grasp of my previous partner. When the music came to an end, Mr. Campbell led me back to my seat and complimented me on my progress.

"Thank you, young lady. You show some promise as a dancer."

"Thank you, Mr. Campbell," I answered with delight, "for teaching me the Rhumba."

There was no sign of Whitey when the music echoed around the room for the next dance. But it made no difference, for now I was in demand as a dancing partner. I didn't have to wait long on the girls' bench, risking another encounter with that nasty bully.

"Last waltz ladies and gentlemen!" announced Mrs. Campbell, and there was Harry at my side ready to dance. We moved around the ballroom in silence, as was required by our teachers (no talking or small talk was allowed), but we did share shy smiles. Harry's grin betrayed slight amusement but mine was full of gratitude. The dance came to an end and he led me back to the bench to collect my coat and handbag.

"I'll walk you home just in case your admirer is waiting outside," he announced with a grin.

"Thanks, Harry" I answered almost casually, before catching myself in alarm at my ignorance. I had not yet been taught this lesson by Nancy. How should I respond? I continued a bit cautiously. "If you're sure it's not out of the way for you."

"Ah no luv. It's a nice night for a walk anyway."

Harry wore a lovely, camel-hair overcoat which complimented his blonde hair. *He probably bought it in New York,* I thought, as there was nothing like it in any of our city shops. We strolled slowly under a bright, star-filled sky, retracing my earlier steps back to my street, with the addition of a detour which added more time to get to know each other.

He made me laugh when he confessed to telling Whitey that I was his girlfriend, threatening to rough him up if he bothered me again. He asked about my family, and I asked where he lived. We discovered that we had probably played together as children in Latham Street, where he had lived as a child and where I went frequently to visit my grandma.

As my house came into sight, we stepped into the alley. He put his arms around me, squeezing me tight before giving me a light kiss on the cheek.

"You're my pocket Venus," he declared. "I'll take you to the pictures on Friday if you want?"

"That would be smashing," I answered eagerly, "but you will have to come to the house so my mother can meet you, if that's alright?"

"No problem, luv. I'll see you at six on Friday."

I thought I was in love!

When Harry joined his ship the following week, I knew that it would not be long until we were together again. He made short, regular trips between Liverpool and New York, with a few days on shore in Liverpool. I looked forward to his funny letters and tried my best to make my letters to him, just as witty.

One day Ma discovered that Harry was three years older than me. She bided her time until he came to the house one day to take me to the pictures.

"Harry," she announced, "I don't want you coming around here again. You are quite a bit older than Maire and a lot more worldly. You had better stay away until she turns eighteen."

Harry stood quietly; head bowed slightly while I pleaded with Ma to change her mind. She refused to budge. Adding to the embarrassment, my big sister Joan appeared in the room having been drawn towards the commotion. She joined in with Ma, humiliating Harry by making spiteful remarks about his fancy camel-hair coat. He stood stoically for a while, before giving me a faint smile before making his way to the door.

We were both devastated but my family's tactics were successful, and Harry no longer came to call on me. For many weeks we had no communication, then one day an envelope with a foreign stamp arrived in my letter box. It was addressed to me and had been posted from South America where Harry's ship was in dock. He had written to let me know that he had signed on to a new ship and would be away for six months. In accordance with my family's wishes, he added, this would be his last contact with me.

I was heartbroken. *If only I could run away to a place where Ma could never reach me!* At sixteen, there was nothing I could do except to keep working at the chocolate factory where I still had my lovely friend Nancy.

Meanwhile, I would spend my time at Campbell's School of Ballroom Dance. I had many more dances to learn...and now my sights were set on the biggest ballroom in the city: the *Locarno*.

IT'S A CIRCUS AT THE LOCARNO!

"Go home luv and come back when you're eighteen!" shouted the ticket seller from the security of the glass-windowed booth. I watched in horror as his large, meaty-looking hands appeared through the small opening at the base of the window and stubby fingers thrust my money back toward me. I had been turned away from one of Liverpool's biggest and grandest dance halls, the Locarno.

My friends who had succeeded where I had not, in accordance with our prearranged plan, skipped away through the ornate doors into the ballroom as I pocketed my half -crown. They laughed sympathetically, waving goodbye as I watched wistfully from the lobby. Gaining admittance to the Locarno dance hall had been my obsession since turning seventeen and an important goal together with the completion of my shorthand and typing classes. I hoped that these efforts would be important milestones on my way to independence.

I had been fascinated with the grandiosity of this ballroom since I was twelve years old when I was invited here to cheer on the girl next door, as she competed in the final round of a beauty contest. Now, while I stood alone in the foyer recovering from the shock of rejection, my eyes rested upon the decorated ceiling with its parade of miniature plaster elephants, tail to trunk, marching around the circular room. I recalled the history of this legendary hall, which my elderly uncles related to me when I was a young child.

The building which housed the famous Locarno ballroom was the result of an eccentric Victorian entrepreneur's impossible dream of building an indoor circus, a 'hippodrome' in Liverpool. Copied in part from the design of the Colosseum, the ancient amphitheater in Rome, he created a stable for larger animals like elephants and tigers below ground, with a lift to transport them to the circus ring for performances.

As a circus, the Locarno had become a wonderful place of entertainment for the people of Liverpool. Teams of beautiful girls rode bare-back horses, while clowns entertained the children. I wondered if Annie Oakley, the famous sharpshooter from America ever performed here. I questioned my uncles to see if they knew what had happened to the old circus, why it closed, but I never got a complete answer. They just shook their heads in puzzlement while mumbling something about "Money" and "The Depression".

The original Victorian décor, however, had been carefully preserved to this day. New wood floors had been installed for dancing, above the space where large animals once rested. The original balcony with its ornate gilt and velvet seating, appeared to be untouched by time. Teeny boppers who, a bit older than me perhaps, had somehow finagled their way inside, now powdered their cheeks in the still-elegant, Regency-style dressing room. They stood in front of the same gilt trimmed mirrors where circus performers, in another era, had put finishing touches to their makeup before entering the ring.

But not this teeny bopper! I had been thwarted by the irascible gatekeeper. My efforts to gain entrance to the Locarno ballroom had become a weekly, interminable struggle. As each Thursday came around, I studiously examined weekly magazines like the *Reveille* or *Woman's Own*, copying those hair and fashion styles which I thought would make me seem more mature than my seventeen years. Then disguising myself further with strategic applications of make-up, I dolloped Max Factor pancake on my face and generously painted my lips 'puce' pink, before taking the local bus that evening to "The Loc" to try again.

On this night, I had entered through the ornate glass doors into the lobby, while trying to manage a casual stroll in a pair of my big sisters high-heeled shoes. Stopping briefly to take a deep breath and pull myself together, I carefully walked toward the glass ticket kiosk. Inside dwelled that unyielding clod of a ticket taker who doubled as gatekeeper to that hallowed hall. There was no need to show identification, because no alcohol was served, and nobody had heard of an ID back in the fifties. The management simply required their patrons to appear to be at least eighteen...my problem was that I looked a lot younger.

Keeping my head turned, as if to watch the orchestra musicians enter carrying their instruments, and in an attempt to hide my baby face, I casually pushed my half-crown piece through the glass hole in the window of the kiosk. My heart fluttered as a moment went by, then another. I could see my friends who had gained entrance, waiting by the door to the dance floor, hoping that I would be joining them. Bernie waved at me and gave me a thumbs-up.

I was sure that tonight was the night that I would be successful. Then I heard a clatter as the half-crown spun across the counter, tossed back at me by the merciless ticket seller. Thwarted again! The crowd behind me stomped and heaved forward as I was ejected from the line. I looked over at the door in time to see Bernie pretending to wipe tears from her eyes while Nora and Margie sadly waved goodbye. I wearily turned and exited the lobby into the street.

Sitting on the upper deck of the bus as I returned home, I was dejected, but not done. Determined to be luckier next time, I knew that if I stayed the course that I would wear him down. But how old would I be by that time? *"Thirty, with half a dozen kids?",* I thought angrily. My thoughts went back and forth until I became exhausted. Tomorrow was another day, and I would come up with a better plan.

In the assumption that someone who looked like Elizabeth Taylor would never be turned away from the ballroom, I returned the following week with a big beauty spot penciled onto my cheek and heavy mascara on my lashes. With a barely audible grunt, the ticket seller waved me away. Did he recognize me by now?

The following Thursday, I tried to look like Lauren Bacall, combing my hair into a wave which swooped down across my forehead to cover one eye. I sauntered up to casually place my half-crown on the counter while trying to imagine that this was how Lauren would behave if she were in my place. I was met with the usual response:

"Get out of here kid!"

Every week I tried a new tactic yet each one was met with the same blunt refusal. I decided the following Thursday would be my last attempt. I broke the news to Bernie.

"This is it!" I said to her as we walked home from work together. "If I don't get in next time, I'm giving up."

"Ah, well, I don't blame ye," she answered, "but if ye must, then give it the grand effort!"

"What d'ye think I've been doin' all these weeks, twiddlin' me thumbs?"

"Ye've not tried goin' in late when everyone is dashin' in at once, getting 'im all flustered."

"Yer right Bernie. I'll give that a try."

As usual when Thursday evening came around, I took the number 14 bus to the Locarno with the girls. I waited outside in the street while they went inside to buy their tickets.

"See you in there!" yelled Bernie as she disappeared into the lobby.

I waited until a crowd had begun to build up in line before entering the queue, jumping into their midst before the next group arrived. Like a stow-away, I was well hidden amongst the would-be dancers, as they pushed and shoved me on my way to the ticket kiosk.

My nerves had gotten the better of me, now that the dreaded moment was within reach having publicly sworn that this was going to be the last time. I could hardly hold on to my money, I was sweating so hard.

Before I knew it I was there at the kiosk. It was now or never!

I gritted my teeth, readying myself for a final rejection as the crowd behind me jostled and pushed, almost knocking me over. Barely holding my ground, I pushed my half-crown through the slot in the window and waited. The money disappeared. What had happened? The crowd began shouting at the delay: "Get a move on Luv!" "What's the hold up?" I was stunned for the moment, unable to react. Yet curiously, there was no immediate rejection of my half crown. Bending over to peer into the kiosk, I glanced quizzically at the ticket seller. He was a big fellow with a thick neck, on top of which sat a pleasant, acne-scarred face. A boxer now or in his former life, his bulbous nose and cauliflower ears gave away his former profession.

"Persistence pays off luv!" he said with a big grin, as he pushed a ticket through the slot with one burly hand.

I stood in shock until someone in the crowd behind me, began to grumble impatiently,

"What's the bloody hold-up?!"

"Thanks, luv," I replied to the ticket seller, "you took me off guard there for a minute."

"Ah, well," he answered, "go and enjoy yerself!"

I was in! Carried along again by the rowdy crowd, I entered the ballroom through the ornate glass doors. I was ecstatic, drunk with success as I made my way to the lady's powder room. I hoped to catch sight of my friends before the dancing began but they had been watching me enter.

"Ah, look what the cat has dragged in!" yelled Bernie, waving from the far corner of the room.

"I can't believe it," shouted Nora, "they must be mad letting that one in!"

It was their usual sarcasm, but at that moment, I wanted only congratulations. They must have noticed my reaction.

"Just having yer on, girl. I'm chuffed that you made it this time," Nora added, placing her arm around my shoulder to give me a big kiss on the cheek just as Margie came over to give me a hug.

Bernie stood apart from the others clapping her hands in applause.

"They can't keep a good woman down!" she proclaimed exultantly. "I knew you'd make it tonight".

"I luv yer Liz Taylor eyes!" declared Margie. "Got any more of that mascara with yer?"

"I haven't luv." I answered with a giggle. "I used the last of it, gettin' in 'ere tonight!"

My friends and I were irrepressible as we luxuriated in the glamorous surroundings. Giggling and laughing, we touched up our makeup, swapping earrings and shoes. I felt that anything was possible now that I had finally been admitted to the Locarno.

The sound of musicians tuning up and the sudden vacating of the dressing room brought our hijinks to a stop, as the evening was about to begin.

"Come on, you lot!" commanded Bernie. "Let's get out here and claim that spot under the big clock before anyone else takes it."

We hurried out to the ballroom in time to see the band leader enter the stage. He stood like a male model on the podium in front of his sixteen-piece, tuxedo-clad orchestra. Tall and slender, with a 'continental' complexion and greying hair, his style was that of the silent movie star Rudolph Valentino, complete with slicked-down, center-parted hair. He was handsome in the fashion of the thirties, and when he spoke, his speech sounded plummy and dated, like that of band leaders in days gone by.

"Good evening, Ladies and Gentlemen!" he announced, "and welcome to another night of dancing with Sonny Swann and his Orchestra. We are going to start off with a quickstep to that wonderful tune made famous by Glen Miller, "String of Pearls".

As Sonny 's orchestra struck up the music, the lights in the massive ballroom dimmed, and a mirrored ball which hung from the ceiling made its descent, coming to a stop a few feet above the dancers. It spun around, glittering in the darkened room, scattering flecks across the walls and ceiling. It looked wonderful, like snowflakes falling on the dancers.

My friends and I stood subdued beneath the great ornate clock, watching quietly as a few dancing couples twirled their way around the room counterclockwise to the music. Other small groups of teenage girls, just like us, stood on the crimson carpet which edged the rim of the dance floor, waiting for a dance partner but there were no boys to be seen. What had happened to our knights in shining armor, our Princes Charmings on their milk white steeds?

"Where are they?" I whispered to Bernie.

"Where's who?" she asked.

"All the boys to dance with?"

Bernie let out a laugh and poked me in the ribs with her elbow before replying.

"They're at the pub, dopey! Filling up on 'Dutch courage' to make them brave enough to ask for a dance. Watch out for yerself, 'cos most of them will be drunk when they get here after intermission."

"After intermission!" I repeated. "Who will we dance Rock n' Roll with, then?"

The Locarno was the only formal ballroom in Liverpool that allowed Rock n' Roll during intermission, and only Thursday evenings, which explained its popularity with teenagers.

"We'll dance together!" she answered. "You don't need fancy dance partners for a Rock n' Roll jive."

It didn't really upset me to discover the lack of dancing partners. I was elated just to be inside the spectacular Locarno Ballroom watching the couples—most of who looked like professional dancers—whirl their way around the floor.

Sonny Swann's band played some of my favorite songs that night, such as Cleo Lane's "I'm Beginning to See the Light", and Lena Horne's "Deed I Do", songs that my sisters and I had learned from listening to radio shows at home. We knew the words to those numbers by heart and would present them in a pretend London Palladium production to our parents. We practiced for weeks in advance to the delight of our mother.

"That's a smashing show," she would say adding, "all we need is Fred Astaire to walk in the door to put the finishing touch on it!" Our serious Dad would wink at her before commenting,

"Listen to you Missus! You've got these girls as daft as yourself."

An announcement by Sonny Swann interrupted my reveries and brought me back to the present, back to the Locarno.

"Take your partners, ladies and gents, for the last dance before intermission!" he announced grandly. "Our very own Cecil Shawcross will perform his rendition of "Blue Moon", made famous by the one and only Billie Holiday."

Many of the dancers looked a bit weary after dancing non-stop all evening. They were ready for a slow dance now, not to mention having a full rest at intermission. Sonny had outdone himself this evening. They had played the Latin music that I was introduced to when I was at Campbell's School of Dancing, churning out the Tango, the Rhumba and the Cha-cha-cha, one after another.

During intermission, many couples left the floor and made their way to the balcony for refreshments, giving us four girls an opportunity to leave our corner of the ballroom. We were able to stroll around the room to examine other areas of this magnificent old structure. As we were lingering in front of the orchestra area, we saw a group of five teenage boys about my age enter through a side door and walk onto the stage. They were dressed alike in black pants and plaid shirts. Sort of scrawny looking, with longish hair, they seemed bewildered as they looked out over the gigantic ballroom.

"What do you think they're up to?" Margie asked.

"They must be the musical group that's going to be playing during intermission." I replied.

The nervous looking lads then headed back to the exit door where their gear had been stacked in a pile. They had probably taken a taxi here and now sweated and strained to carry their strange looking instruments into the hall. Their activity had caught the attention of Bernie whose face lit up.

"Let's go over and talk to them while they're setting up," Bernie suggested, as she pulled me along with her.

"Hey lads, do youse need a hand?" she shouted, as the lads struggled with a giant wooden box like a tea chest, from which extended a long mop handle.

We gathered around the stage watching the lads, while trying to guess what kind of music they would be playing. Margie thought she knew and called out to them.

"Are youse lads a skiffle group like Lonnie Donegan?"

"Yer right there luv," replied the tallest lad, who looked slightly older than the others.

"Will yer play some of 'is songs?"

"Some of 'is and some of our own luv."

"What's the name of yer group luv?"

"The Quarrymen," he answered with a laugh. "Remember that name! We're going to be famous, bigger than Lonnie."

"Oh yeah, with bells on luv!" responded Bernie with a giggle. "Yez've gotta get yerselves a Yankee agent first, before yez get famous."

Everyone laughed, not to make fun of them, but knowingly. We were amused at the idea that any local lad of our age could become famous, not that we wanted to burst anyone's bubble. We all needed a dream, a way to escape the factory life. My private dream was to escape to Malibu Beach and find work as a secretary, far away from the conveyor belt. At the same time, it was common knowledge around Liverpool that a band had to be good enough to appear on television, or get invited to perform in America, for a chance to become famous.

The lads finished setting up and began playing. Two or three of the younger fellers stood in the back, playing guitars, while the older feller who had done all the talking slapped the string on the tea-chest. A young drummer completed the group as they played a few of our favorites. They belted out such popular hits as "Rock Island Line", "Does Your Chewing Gum Lose Its Flavor on the Bedpost Overnight?", "Gamblin' Man", "My Old Man's a Dustman", and "Putting on the Style".

The formal ballroom began to fill up with young teenagers bopping to the beat, pushing aside the formal dancing couples. The skiffle music gave everyone a chance to cut loose and dance a bit more freely. Girls who had been standing around all evening waiting for a partner, peeled themselves off the wall to team up and dance together, while others danced solo in a world of their own.

"Are yez all having a good time?" shouted the tall skinny feller who we later found out was the leader of the group. Female voices throughout the hall screamed back, "Yeeesss!"

"OK folks we're going to finish up with that old chestnut, "The Sheik of Araby". If you've enjoyed me and the lads, please put in a request to invite us back again! Thank you all from The Quarrymen."

By this time, the floor had grown dense and rowdy with the addition of young men who had newly arrived from the pubs. They ambled around in a daze trying to 'chat-up' groups of girls who were dancing together. Some got lucky with the promise of a waltz later in the evening, but for most it was resounding rejection.

It all came to an end as Sonny Swan's band marched back to the stage and began playing Glen Miller's, "In the Mood". Teeny boppers scattered, the dance floor once again filled with stodgy fox-trotting couples, and The Quarrymen packed up their equipment. Bernie walked over to say goodbye to them.

"Yer group was smashing", she said to the leader, "Youse have got a great sound. Hope yez come back again next week. What's yer name luv?"

"John," he answered. "Thanks for the compliment, luv. We hope we can come back again too! But ye haven't got rid of us yet. Management says we can stay and have a dance as part of the payment deal! Not that any of us know how to waltz," he added with a grin, "but we'll give it a try."

"That's good," she answered. "If you're gonna' be around, me mates and me will be under the big clock over there."

By the time our group of girls had assembled again in the usual place, Nora was already up dancing with a nice looking, sober feller. The ballroom post intermission was jammed with teenage couples trying to hook up before the evening ended.

They either slew-footed around the floor or stood in one spot moving in circles, making it almost impossible for the more refined semi-professional dancers to perform their fancy footwork. Bernie was asked to dance with a fellow whose hair was almost as red as hers, but who was shy a couple of inches in height. She had grown like a weed over the past year and now towered over most of her dance partners in mild but amusing embarrassment to both. Margie disappeared into the arms of a fair-haired boy, leaving me standing alone under the clock. But not for long.

"Do you want to dance this one luv?"

It was the boy who had played guitar in the back row of the skiffle group. He looked noticeably young, and his cheeky face belied his nice manners.

"I don't mind." I answered as nonchalantly as possible, which was the "cool" way teenaged girls responded in the Fifties. He took my hand and led me onto the dance floor.

At first, he made the usual conversation as we attempted to move around the crowded floor.

"Do you live around 'ere luv?"

"No. I live by the football ground in Anfield."

"Aw, a Liverpool supporter, are you?"

"No, and not an Everton one either." I answered. "Who do you support?"

"I'm an Evertonian. D'ye come 'ere often?"

"Every Thursday." I answered, omitting the fact that tonight was the first time the management had allowed me to enter the ballroom. He stumbled over my feet and blushed in embarrassment.

"Sorry luv."

"That's alright." I replied.

He was quiet after that. I tried to make conversation.

"You've got a smashing group there," I continued. "Everyone loved yer music."

"Thanks, luv."

He went quiet again and looked nervously around the ballroom giving the impression that he was uncomfortable at not knowing the dance steps.

He didn't ask my name and I didn't ask his. We were both shy, and it is well known that two shy people do not make a good match because somebody must be brave enough to speak up. We shuffled around the Locarno until the dance ended and he walked me back to the clock.

"Thanks for the dance luv. Sorry about tripping you up." he said.

"Not to worry, luv," I answered, "better luck next time."

Then he disappeared into the crowd.

My friends stared at me with sly smiles as they moved in to surround me.

"The state of you, dancing with one of those skiffle group fellers!" exclaimed Nora.

"Yea, he looked like a nice young feller. Not shaving yet though," added Margie with a giggle.

"Ah now," said Bernie. "Yer won't listen to these two after ye've seen the couple of drips who are walking them home. But to be honest with yer, Maire, he was a bit young."

As the last waltz began to play, there was a rush onto the floor as the "Dutch courage" kicked in for those fellers who had sat most of the night in the pub. It was their last chance to seduce one of the naïve young girls, desperate for a boyfriend, into letting them walk her home. A stop at the 'Chip Shop' to buy "*four penneth*" of chips, and they were on their way to getting a date for the weekend.

Many of the professional style ballroom dancers had already left for the evening, taking with them the international flair and some of the feeling of wonderment. Sonny Swann's orchestra was beginning to sound like an unwound record, slowly coming to its tipsy conclusion. Bernie gave me a nod indicating that it was time for us to leave.

It was almost eleven o'clock when we jumped on the last bus going in our direction. Because it was the last bus to leave town, it only went as far as the depot in Penny Lane, but lucky for us it passed through our neighborhood on its way. The packed bus smelled of cigarette smoke, stale beer and fish and chips as it swayed along through the quiet streets of the city. As it was standing room only, Bernie and I hung on to the overhead straps as the bus lurched around corners until we reached Oakfield road.

It had been impossible to talk on the bus ride back to Anfield, but we still had a distance to walk before reaching our street.

"I'm made up that I got into the Loc at last," I said, "we'll have some smashing laughs there, won't we?"

Bernie didn't answer right away. Glancing over at me, she rolled her eyes.

"You might but not me." she said quietly.

"Why not you?"

"Because I'm not going there again."

"I'm head and shoulders over most of the lads in there," she added sadly, "and it's hard for me to get a dance. Besides, I don't like those waltzes and foxtrots anyway."

What could I say? It was true, she was bigger and stronger than most of the lads in Liverpool. I felt guilty when I realized that she had been holding off on telling me until I could get into the Locarno by myself.

"You'll grow into it, Bernie," I said. "You're just awkward right now but before long, you will look elegant like one of those French models."

She grinned at me. "I'll have to wait and see."

We promised that we would go to parties together, especially those where we could dance to Rock n' Roll music. Perhaps when we turned eighteen, we could visit some of the new night clubs that were sprouting up in the city.

It had been a successful night for me because I had finally got into "The Loc"!

All I needed now was to learn how to talk to a boy...

A CHEESE SANDWICH
FOR JOHN LENNON

I
t's raining in Liverpool on Monday, February 1962. It began to pour down right after Christmas and has refused to stop. Rain has been falling for days on end, in the streets and on the rooftops. The sound of milk bottles jangling on the stone doorstep awakened me early this morning and hoping the rain had ceased during the night, I glance over at the metal bucket sitting in a corner of the bedroom. It is positioned to catch raindrops coming in from a hole in the roof of our rented house, which our skinflint landlord refuses to fix. Perhaps the downpour has finally stopped? But no, the bucket is half full again. The rain is still at it.

Day after day, it has rained with no break. It eases up into a drizzly mist for brief periods, teasing us into believing this is the end, before gathering its strength for the next onslaught. I get out of bed and walk across the room to stand by the window, where I watch numbly as water streams across the cracked windowpanes of our Victorian terraced house then down into the street below. Small rivulets have gathered at the top of the sloping street, combining to create a great gully which channels into grey, granite gutters. Downhill it runs, collecting old cigarette packages, bus tickets and an assortment of twigs on its way.

I am mentally preparing myself for a mad dash through the deluge to catch the local bus to my job, but I feel starved for sunshine! I require some semblance of it, if only a reminder of sunny, blue skies. Caribbean music will do. I know exactly where to find it—the Jacaranda Club!

It is one of those new-style coffee clubs that arrived in Liverpool a few years ago, about the same time I became a teenager. These fellers, entrepreneurs, buy up ruined old cellar buildings in the city, even ones that must be hundreds of years old. They fix them up with a bit of paint, set up an espresso machine then hire rock bands, which are ten-a-penny in this city. The Jacaranda is a great place to hang out any time of the year but especially so on wet, wintery nights.

Fate has provided me with an inside track to most night clubs in Liverpool, despite my shy demeanor. I have had to look for an evening job to make ends meet, something the weekly pay from my full-time day job working as a tailor, cannot do. God love her, my poor mother is unable to work full time these days, so I must support her and myself, the remains of our family. She had a nervous breakdown after my dad died, just as the war came to an end. A couple of years later, my eldest sister got married and moved to Canada, so it is up to me to make sure the rent is paid, and there is enough coal to keep us warm and dry.

My friend Bernadette works for a man named Jim Ireland who is one of the new entrepreneurs. She mentioned that he was looking for a weekend waitress at their very elegant, downtown coffee bar, and if I was interested, she'd put in a good word for me. Go ahead,

I told her before rushing over there as fast as I could for an interview.

The uniformed commissioner at the entrance to the coffee bar, looked so stern just like one of those guards outside Buckingham Palaces. He was staring straight ahead, ignoring me and everything else when I arrived, and making me almost lose my nerve. It was a 'do or die' situation and I needed to psych myself up to appear confident. I recalled the instructions our drama teacher at Stanley Park Secondary Modern drilled into us: *"Inhabit the character you wish to portray."* It was meant to be a bit of advice for fifteen-year old school leavers before being sent out to work in grimy factories, but it was worth a try now.

Taking a deep breath, I pulled myself up to expand every one of my sixty inches.

"I'm here for an interview," I said, putting on my best Princess Margaret smile. He smiles back at me and swings open the large glass and chrome door.

"Mr. Ireland is waiting for you in his office, straight back there. Good luck, luv," he adds with a wink, "you'll do fine."

Jim Ireland was seated at a desk crunching numbers on one of those hand operated, adding machines, extruding streams of paper tape. I knocked on the open door to let him know that I had arrived while giving him the once over. Nice-looking for his age, which was a lot older than me, he was perhaps in his late thirties with thinning fair hair and a moustache. He had been frowning with concentration but stopped to look up at the sound of my knock.

"Sorry to interrupt, Mr. Ireland. I'm Maire Mac, a friend of Bernie Murphy's, here to interview for the weekend waitress job."

"Oh right, luv. Have a seat. I've got to finish this up, then I'll be with you straight away."

Taking a seat, I looked around while all sorts of thoughts raced through my head. I felt like I had entered a different country, one with bare, teak wood floors and shiny Scandinavian décor. I worried that he would ask me, during the interview, what my father did when he was alive, just like the stuck-up old biddies in the Bon Marche and Lewis's department stores. When I proudly told them that he was a dock worker, they always responded with, *Sorry dear, we don't hire people of your class in this establishment.*

I could see this place was different, very modern, at least in décor and Mr. Ireland had hired my good friend Bernie. Maybe he would give me a chance! My thoughts were interrupted by the gentleman himself.

"Have you tried our coffee yet?

"No, not yet but everyone tells me that it's fantastic!"

He was amused by my response and a faint smile crept across his face.

"Let me get you a cup before we begin. You can tell me what you think." He disappeared from the room for a moment, then came back holding a glass cup and saucer brimming with white, steaming froth. I could not contain my delight at the sight of it, grinning and sipping at the delicious drink as he began the interview.

"So, my employee, Bernadette Murphy told you about the job opening, did she?"

"Yes, we're best friends. We went to school together and live on the same street."

"She recommended you for the job. Are you a good worker like her?"

"Absolutely! We trained together, picking spuds in the summer when we were kids!" I answered with a laugh.

"That's good to know because we'll be relying a lot on our staff in the next few months as we expand our business. Me and my partner, Stan Roberts, who you will meet eventually, are planning on opening some nightclubs. You and Bernie will fill in at some of those places when we need an extra hand. Do you think you can handle the confusion?

"Definitely! I'll work wherever you need me".

"You'll be running into some crazy characters such as bartenders and a lot of musicians. Will you be alright with that?"

"No problem. My relatives are pub musicians and they're mad." I answered, trying to appear confident.

"Right then, we'll give it a try. Come to work with Bernie next Saturday morning. She will fix you up with a uniform and help you with the paperwork. You can go out onto the floor after lunch."

"Aw thanks, Mr. Ireland," I said, "I won't let you down."

My friend had already filled me in on the pay and the perks, so my new boss and I shook hands on it, and I started work the following Saturday.

I am chuffed! I love my part-time job working Thursday and Friday nights and all-day Saturday at the exclusive Mallorca Espresso coffee bar on Tarleton

Street. As a waitress, I wear a pink uniform, with a black, French-maid style, apron, along with my own high heels and black nylon stockings. It's like having access to my own magic carpet, which carries me away from my days on the assembly line of a clothing factory and into the glamorous world of jazz and rock music. I am called a floater which means that I fill in whenever a staff emergency arises in one of the clubs. Before long, I am a familiar face in those venues, serving coffee, pulling pints, checking coats, or taking tickets at the entrance.

But tonight, is my night off and I have a plan to shake off the rain, dancing to Caribbean music. Telephones have not yet reached our humble neighborhood, but my friends and I all live on the same street. I stop at Nora's house on the way home from work.

"Let's go to the Jacaranda tonight!"

"Oh God! I would luv to get out tonight, Maire, but I dare not risk it. If our Joe or Eddy find out I am going dancing, they'll beat me up. Then I'll have to stay home from work with a couple of black eyes."

Her father and two brothers watch her every move. They are terrified that some man will steal her virginity and shame the family, so they forbid her to go dancing. Nora and I have hatched a plan to counteract their scheme. On clubbing nights, she lies, telling them she's attending a church meeting.

"Ta-ra," she says casually, "I'm going to bible study."

"Another one?" they ask quizzically, "you'll be the second, bloody Joan of Arc before ye know it, girl!"

The men approve of church meetings and wave benignly as she leaves home wearing her plain work clothes. But there is a detour to my house where I have a package hidden away, stuffed with her dancing clothes and mascara. Sneaking out to go dancing takes careful planning but tonight there's not enough time. I will have to try Bernie.

"Ah, I wish I could go with you but I'm babysitting tonight".

I try Elaine. No, she is washing her hair. Maureen? No, she has a typing class tonight.

I cannot be deterred and make my mind up to go alone.

"Are you going out in this rain?" Ma asks, when she sees me coming down the stairs all togged up in my clubbing clothes, a new sweater and stiletto heels.

"Yes, I am."

"You need your head feeling."

"Maybe so, but I can't shut my life off just because it's pissing down."

"Don't come crying to me when you come down with pneumonia."

"Ah now, I know ye wouldn't let me croak! Don't wait up for me." I grab my coat and slam the door shut behind me quickly, but not fast enough for her to shout a warning.

"Half past eleven, no later, madam!"

Then a short walk over to Holy Trinity Church where I wait for a bus. There are half a dozen people ahead of me in line, all with umbrellas hoisted overhead. The blowing wind forces us to bump into each other, entangling the spokes from our brollies as we cluster close together to form a weather barrier.

There is no chance of flashers in the bus queue during this bad weather, but on a fine evening you'd better watch out for them in their raincoats, lurking in the darkness. It has happened to me a couple of times, while waiting in line. Perhaps it is the proximity of bodies that triggers the action of a small tap on the shoulder. I turn around thinking it's my friend, only to see the overcoat fly open and some weirdo stood there grinning. Not tonight though. We are all respectable, orderly, and wet.

A green double-decker bus appears out of the darkness and comes to a stop. I hop on and climb to the upper deck. It is empty except for two passengers who are already seated. They are puffing away on their Woodbine cigarettes and reading the Liverpool Echo newspaper whose headlines blare out, THIRTY-FIVE THOUSAND WORKERS UNEMPLOYED IN LIVERPOOL. I am lucky to have one job, let alone two!

The upper deck of the bus smells bad with a combination of rain-soaked wool, stale tobacco, and diesel fuel. The floor is messy, strewn with cigarette butts, empty fish and chip wrappers and rainwater carried in on Wellington boots. I don't care, I am simply happy to have a seat to myself where I can gaze through the steamy window and let my thoughts drift away to a vision of palm trees overlooking a bright blue sea.

"Central Station, luv!" yells the bus conductor up the stairs, arousing me from my daydream. With an assortment of squeaks and grinds, the bus groans to a halt. I descend the stairs along with a few more clubbers who boarded the bus while I was in the tropics.

An old couple are down on the platform, struggling to get their suitcase out from the storage area under the stairs. They are blocking the exit and no-one can get off the bus.

"Sorry luvs," the gent says, "the missus and me are holding youse all up."

"Ah, it's alright," someone answers, speaking for all of us who are backed up on the stairs.

"Will someone down there lend a hand before they miss their bloody train?"

A mod couple are ahead of me, perhaps on their way to the Jacaranda club too. The girl pokes her feller in his ribs with her elbow, indicating he should help. He jumps down and easily retrieves the suitcase. It is like pulling the plug from a drain as we all go flooding out onto the street. I walk up Bold Street, take a sharp right on Slater Street, and I am there, knocking on the door of the Jacaranda Club.

Patrons are not free to open the door and walk into the Jacaranda Club. There is a discreet screening process done by a hired doorman to avoid trouble. The club sells no alcohol, so they turn drunken patrons away, as well as ladies of the night and lads who love fighting. I cannot see a doorman here tonight, so I wave through the glass window to catch the eye of the owner, who waves back as he walks over to unlock the door.

Short and chubby, with a shock of black, curly hair and rosy-apple cheeks, Alan Williams looks like a refugee from a Charles Dickens play. He is another friend of my employers, Roberts and Ireland, and by default, he's my friend too. He runs this club with his wife Beryl, who is a beautiful Asian woman.

"Where's the doorman?" I ask.

"It's Monday, remember? His night off. The band's off tonight too."

"Ach no, I forgot," I gasp. "I was looking forward to swaying to the sound of steel drums."

Alan laughs, making his eyes twinkle like two pieces of shiny, black coal.

"No Caribbean music tonight, luv. You'll have to make do with a little Rock and Roll music, played by Scousers in wet overcoats."

I am really bummed out when I hear guitar sounds, drifting up from the cellar stage. My heart was set on hearing music of the Caribbean, and it will take a lot to win me over. I will cheer myself up with one of Beryl's famous, toasted cheese sandwiches.

These are not the usual soggy specimens consisting of fake cheese between two pieces of pre-sliced bread. Not at all. Beryl's masterpieces are open-faced and so crunchy, they must be eaten with a knife and fork. She first cuts a thick slice of fresh bread and toasts it under the grill in the small kitchen. Then she loads it up with good English cheese, usually Red Leicester, cut from a huge wedge. She tops that with thin slices of tomato, before returning it to the grill. The cheese bubbles up, oily and moist until it drips down the sides, while the tomato cooks just enough for it to singe around the edges, browning slightly. I do not know where she got the idea for them, but they are to die for.

Alan and I laugh as I shake the rain from my umbrella, before parking it in the coat check.

"Seriously though," he says, "these blokes are good. I should know because I used to manage them. They're broke after getting back from working a gig in Germany, so I hired them for Monday nights."

"Ah well then, we'd better give them a chance. A leg up for local lads."

I feel right at home in the Jacaranda Club where it is dark and mysterious. Alan must have visited Vienna or perhaps Budapest, places in Europe well known for their coffee houses, before returning with a blueprint for his own place. The seating area is so cozy in the club and no bigger than a decent sized living-room with everything painted black. The lighting is diffused and seating areas low to the ground. It is very private for a public venue. Numerous romantic liaisons are carried on, discreetly hidden in dimly lit corners, but being British, there is no public touching allowed apart from hand-holding and a peck on the cheek.

The Jacaranda is frequented by young people in their late teens or early twenties. Guests are mainly university students, musicians, or young fruit importers from Spain. Local artists and poets flock to the club, like homing pigeons coming in to roost so it is not unusual for me to come home with a charcoal portrait in my bag or the occasional poem. I like the atmosphere here with everyone getting along, except for the time a contingent of the Israeli navy came to town.

Our country, Great Britain, maybe out of guilt for all the trouble they caused over there, gave the emerging nation a couple of submarines. Officers and crew stayed in Liverpool for training, but their timing coincided with that of a group of young Egyptian medical students, sent by President Abdul Nassar to study at Liverpool University.

Fights broke out whenever these notorious enemies encountered each other, and poor Alan Williams, who had tried to be his own United Nations by inviting them all to the Jacaranda Club, was at his wits end. Local patrons of the club such as Liverpool lads joined in the melee, indignant that having recently ended years of their own war, they now had to witness another country's war right there on the dance floor of a beloved club. It all came to an end and peace ensued within the Jacaranda Club, when the Israeli navy sailed home in their second-hand ships.

Tonight, I take a seat in one of the nooks across from a serious-looking fellow in a tweed jacket. He is preoccupied with sketching something on a large pad but looks up briefly to give me a silent nod. I smile over at him and prepare to order my toasted cheese sandwich and an espresso. The music has stopped echoing up from the basement and I realize that it must be intermission for the band. My eyes drift around the room and soon alight on a fellow I have never seen here before.

Dressed in black, with a leather jacket, he attracts my attention because of his unusual behavior. He moves around the room slowly, stopping briefly beside each of the nooks for a moment, to whisper something to each cluster of guests. They respond by digging into their pockets before placing a few coins into his hand. Nonchalantly he moves on to stop at the next nook. He slips stealthily in beside the guests, then repeats his routine. It dawns on me what he is doing. I have seen it done before.

He looks across the room, catches me watching him then quickly comes over to ask me something.

"Hiya luv," he says. "You haven't got a couple of pence to spare, have yer? I'm just short of the price for one of those delicious looking, cheese sandwiches." His voice sounds deep and dozy.

I cannot help but laugh at him.

"And how much did you start out with, luv?" I ask as he grins at me.

Realizing the game is up, he responds bashfully.

"Ah, go wan, girl."

He is very thin. *God knows when he last had a good meal.* He seems perplexed, wondering what I am going to do next.

"You know, luv," I tell him, "it's your lucky night. I'm ordering one for myself so I will order an extra one for you. The 'sarnie' is on me!"

"Aw, thanks luv, I'm made up!"

"I'll call you over when it's ready," I say. "What's your name?"

"John" he answers, grinning from ear to ear as heads back across the room to his mates.

Ten minutes later, two luscious, Red Leicester, toasted cheese sandwiches arrive.

"Hey, John," I shout, standing up to wave. "Your sandwich is here!"

Three long strides and he is right here. Rubbing his hands together, he grins at the delicious sight.

"Aw, smashing, luv," he says. "Ye're saving me life 'ere!"

He sits down in the nook next to me, then picking up the knife and fork, he begins to eat.

"Hey John, I'm not trying to get rid of you, luv," I tell him, "but you can take your sandwich back to your table with your mates if you'd like."

"Bad idea, girl," he answers with a grin. "The lads 'll scarf it up in no time. I'll just stay out of sight here until I've eaten it, if ye don't mind."

"I don't mind," I say, "whatever floats your boat."

In silence, we attack our sandwiches until John suddenly sits back. Hands across his belly, he lets out a sigh.

"Aw God, that hit the spot!"

"Smashing, aren't they? This place is well known for their cheese sandwiches."

"I wouldn't know, girl. I've been in Germany for a while so I 'm not up on all the clubs in town."

"Oh!" I say, as the light goes on in my head. "You must be one of the lads that Alan mentioned is playing tonight. Are ye?"

"Yeah, that's us."

"What's your group called?"

"The Silver Beatles," he answers, "but we're in between names right now. Looking for a new one 'cos this one hasn't clicked with the club scene."

He looks over to see his mates signaling him that intermission is over.

"I got to get going, luv. See ye later."

"Tara John. I will be down later to check out your group."

I am in no hurry to scarf down my scrumptious supper; besides, I can see that the narrow staircase to the cellar is crammed with people in single file, trying to get down there to listen to this new group. Upstairs has emptied out, with just the artist in the tweed jacket and me remaining in our nook, and a couple of lovebirds across the room. I hear music echoing up and the songs sound familiar. They have opened with Buddy Holly's 'That'll be the Day,' followed by Ray Charles' 'I got a woman', then 'Besame Mucho', and even that music hall chestnut, 'The Sheik of Araby'. They have added their own sound to these hits. but it is unusual for a group to not sing their own songs.

I finish eating and head down to investigate. The cellar is crowded tonight. Its arched, white-washed ceiling is so low that six-footers on the dance floor are forced to duck their heads. Tobacco smoke has turned the already moldy air into a thick blue haze, which hangs over the small dance floor like a rain cloud. It is very steamy too. Sauna-like, with moisture dripping down the windowless, brick walls onto the concrete floor.

John is with his group consisting of three guitarists and a drummer. They are playing on a raised platform in the corner. Alan was right when he told me they were good. The dancers think so too, judging by the huge round of applause that goes up from the crowd as the band finishes the first set. One of their fans shouts above the noise with a request.

"How about one of yer own songs, lads?"

"Yeh," joins in another voice. "Give us 'She Loves You'!"

"Thanks for the requests, everyone," one of them at the mike responds. "For the next set we're going to be playing our own songs. Hope you like them."

They are noticeably confident and at ease with themselves, as well as with the crowd. Lots of joking around goes on between the musicians as well as friendly banter with the crowd, as the group prepares to play the next set. My dance partner who is one of my regular customers from the Mallorca Coffee Bar, tries to guide me away from the crowd, but we can hardly move around on the small floor. *Where did all these people appear from? I didn't see them come in!*

The crowd is going wild as the Silver Beatles sing their own songs, starting with "Love Me Do", then "She Loves You" followed by "P.S. I Love You". The words to the songs are so simple that we all sing along, and the music is catchy in a way that is familiar to us, yet different. It is a Liverpool sound but not entirely, as strains of American rock-n-roll groups like the Everly brothers, wind their way through these original sounds.

"Hey lads," someone in the crowd yells, "have yez got any records out?"

One of the musicians answers him, "We haven't got around to it yet lad."

A rumble of disappointed comments goes up from the crowd. Like me, they have listened to good groups in this city, who never made it to the big time. I have overheard musicians talking in the Mardi Gras Club where I work, about the difficulty Northerners have, trying to break through barriers set up by big London recording studios.

We have managed to edge our way over to a spot in front of the band so I can see John. The cheeky devil winks at me as I dance along to the music. I wink back, giving him a thumbs-up. I wish I could make time stand still—I want the evening to go on forever, but I must get up early for work tomorrow. The set comes to an end amid the roar of the crowd, and I walk over to say goodnight.

"Tara, John," I say, looking over at my new friend. "You fellers are great!"

They all look over, happy with the compliment.

"Alright girl!" shouts the drummer.

"Thanks, luv," comes from the two guitarists in the back.

But John leans over and grabs my arm.

"Thanks girl, see you next Monday." Another wink from my new cheese-sandwich friend, John, and I head upstairs to grab my coat and umbrella.

Still raining buckets, I make a mad dash down Bold Street in my stiletto heels. The last bus passes Central Station at eleven fifteen and if I miss that, it will take me an hour to walk home, and I won't get there until after midnight. If *that* happens, Ma will be waiting for me behind the front door wielding the cast iron poker from the fireplace. She'll threaten me with it and we will struggle. She will eventually calm down but not before she's torn a hank of my hair out and thrown a few prize curses my way. Why does everyone's Ma believe that their daughters will lose their virginity if they stay out after midnight? That is the way it is in this seafaring city.

I reach the bus stop with time to spare. The bus arrives and I climb aboard. The smell of beer and ale hits me like a blast, coming from all the boozers heading home from the pubs. It is standing room only. My feet feel crucified after all that dancing, but it is worth it because I had a ball.

There's a bony old-timer sitting on the aisle seat in front of me muttering to himself, as he eats a few cold, greasy chips out of a newspaper. *I bet he fished them out of the bin. Bless him, poor bugger. He's probably fought in two world wars!* I am feeling benevolent tonight and root a sixpence out of my pocket.

"Ee-ya, luv. Put this in your pocket for tomorrow's chips." His rheumy eyes widen in surprise as he turns to look up.

"Ooh, ta girl!" he says. "This'll get me a bit of cod for me tea tomorrow."

Now I've got him going, he's not going to stop chatting away, a mile a minute.

"Ye probably don't remember when the big chip shop on Stanley Road got bombed by the Gerrie's in the May blitz, do ye luv?"

I shook my head. "No luv, I was only a little nipper at the time."

"Ah well, I'll tell ye." People in Liverpool love to hear stories and the passengers on my bus are no exception, swiveling around in their seats to listen.

"The Luftwaffe came over in the middle of the night and bombed the hell out of us. They just missed the 'chippy' itself, but their storage shed was hit, and spuds went flying everywhere. They were squashed and splattered over the street the next morning, along with all the other damage. Ye couldn't even scrape 'em up for mashed potatoes!" he emphasized for all to hear.

He sat up straight in his seat to glance around, relishing his expanding audience. Laughing out loud gleefully, anticipating the punchline of the story, he opened his mouth to expose one long, front tooth which stood alone, anchored to his bottom gum.

"Well, everyone pitched in and cleaned up the place and by that night the chippy was up and running again. They had to scrounge around all day, begging greengrocers all over the city for spuds to make chips, having lost their own horde in the bombing. Not wanting to deprive any of their customers, they stretched what little they had managed to haul in, by slicing the chips thinner than usual. That night when they opened for business, they put a big sign in the window to let customers know, 'BECAUSE OF HITLER, OUR CHIPS ARE LITTLER!' They had more customers than they could serve with people coming from all over just to see that sign and have a good laugh." By now, the whole bus is laughing, including me.

What a night! I feel great, ready to face anything. The bus reaches my neighborhood and I step out into the cool, night air. It has stopped raining. What more can I wish for? Walking along the moonlit main road to my house on Bala Street, I cannot help smiling to myself as I relive the memorable night at the Jacaranda Club. The group, especially my cheese-sandwich friend, impressed me so much. I say a little prayer for them, hoping they make it to the big time.

I am determined to return next Monday night but life, and all my jobs, get in the way. By the time I got back to the Jacaranda club, the Silver Beatles had moved on to another gig. I never saw them again in person.

The following year, I am working as a nanny in California, when I see my cheese-sandwich friend again. He is right up front on the Ed Sullivan Show as the Beatles are introduced to the world. Yes, it's the same hungry feller, the cheeky bugger from the Jacaranda Club. John Lennon!

Why didn't I ask for an IOU?

ABOUT THE AUTHOR

Maire McMahon is the author of *A Child's Christmas in Liverpool*, a trilogy describing the simple but heartfelt celebrations of the holiday season in post-World War II Britain. Born in Liverpool during the Nazi Blitz, Maire reveals her experiences growing up in a city and community staggering forth from the rubble of conflict with determination and humor.

A Cheese Sandwich for John Lennon is her second book. Based on actual events which she experienced first-hand, the four interlinked stories describe the author's teenage years coming of age during the emerging music scene in 1950's post-war Liverpool.

Maire is currently working on a fiction thriller which is based on a series of chilling and mysterious encounters she experienced while teaching school in a Hindu village on the coast of Guyana, South America.

She lives in Orlando, Florida.

Visit her website at www.maireemcmahon.com for more information about *A Cheese Sandwich for John Lennon* and other projects by Maire McMahon.

Printed in Great Britain
by Amazon

71265039R00043